REAL BASICS

A Beginning ESL Text For Immigrants

S. E. Treadgold

NEW LEAF
ESL MATERIALS   Seattle, Washington

Book design ~ Schlomann Graphic Design • Illustrations ~ Mandy Carter

❖

For my mother, D. Ruth Icenogle Treadgold

❖

Acknowledgments

Thank you to my students, past, present and future.

Thank you to my colleagues, Nicola Andersen, Susan Henderson,
Tammy Herreid, Joyce Kruithof and Diane Riegner, who suggested
exercises, read drafts and offered encouragement.

Thank you to Mandy Carter, for sticking with the project
and sharing her talent.

Thank you to my collaborator, Gretchen Schlomann, of whom
I ask too much and who always delivers the impossible.

E.T.
S.G.D.

15541 Palatine Ave. N, Seattle, WA 98133
www.newleafesl.com

Printed in the United States of America. September 2009

ISBN 0-9663705-2-X

A Note to Teachers

Real Basics is indeed "a beginning ESL text for immigrants." Most students who use it are adults. They are "literate" in English, that is to say they have some familiarity with the sound/sign system, but their grasp may be tenuous. They may have a lot of educational background in their own languages or very little. They may have arrived a few days ago or be immigrants of many years' standing.

For me, Real Basics works best as a lesson-planning guide for teachers, and as a workbook and reference for students. That means that new material is introduced with the texts closed, but it's practiced using exercises from the book or activities from the Teacher's Companion (a compilation of reproducible pictures, cards and games also available from this publisher).

Here's an example of a first lesson:

- A transparency of the Students page from the Companion is projected onto the whiteboard or wall, or photocopies of the same page are distributed.

- The class says the names of the characters a few times and the teacher writes them in a column on the board.

- The teacher gives the information that the class couldn't know, "Carlos is from Mexico. Yuriy is from Ukraine," etc.

- The teacher writes the names of the countries in another column to the right of the first one, leaving a couple of columns' width between them.

- The teacher points to the various countries and the class says them.

- The teacher adds "is" and "from" to the space between the columns and a period after the country column.

- The class practices saying "is" and "from".

- The teacher makes a sentence about one of the characters, pointing with her finger or with a pointer, "Nadia is from Ukraine." and then says the sentence and points to Nadia on the transparency or on her own copy of the page.

- If the class seems ready, she indicates that she'd like a volunteer to come up and make another sentence. If the class doesn't seem ready, she gives another example herself.

- Students from the class come up to the board and point to and say sentences about the characters. Correction is handled at the teacher's discretion.

- The teacher adds "and" and "are" to the board, the "are" placed under "is", and points out "Yuriy and Nadia are from Ukraine."

- If there are two students in the class who are from one of the countries on the board, the teacher adds their names to the first column and students practice saying their names. If they come from a country not already mentioned, it's added to the country column and the class practices saying it.

- The teacher indicates that she'd like a volunteer to make a sentence about these two students and a volunteer does.

- This process continues, adding some or all of the elements the students will need to do the first exercise in the text: "a" in its own column; "man", "woman", "men" and "women" under the country/object column; "he", "she", "they" and "I" in the name column; and "am" under "is" and "are".

  (If the class truly has had no exposure to English, this material may be spread out over a couple of lessons.)

- The class practices saying sentences about the characters and their classmates in pairs at their desks, referring to their copies or the transparency and to the "grid" on the board.

- The activity is expanded to include the names of more students from the class.

- Students are given exercise A to do in class or as homework.

- Perhaps the following day, the class practices with the grid again and then puts exercise A on the board. They consider and correct it.

- The teacher adds "not" to the grid, and so on. . .

If this approach makes sense to you, give it a try. If it doesn't, introduce the material in a way you're comfortable with. Just be sure your students are familiar with the concepts or vocabulary before they have to use it. The "grids" in the text will also be easier for students to understand if they've worked with the format before.

Table of Contents

Pronouns

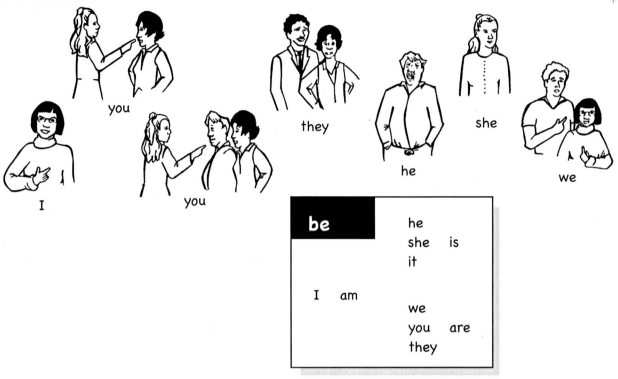

be	
	he
	she is
	it
I am	
	we
	you are
	they

A. Look at the pictures. Fill in the blanks.

  EXAMPLE: Carlos _is_ a man. __He__ _is_ from Mexico.

  1. Nadia _is_ a woman. _She_ _is_ from Ukraine.

  2. Mohammed _is_ a man. _He_ _is_ from Iraq.

  3. Soon _is_ a woman. _She_ _is_ from Korea.

  4. Yuriy _is_ a man. _He_ _is_ from Ukraine.

  5. Jane _is_ a woman. _she_ _is_ from the United States.

2

6. <u>They</u> <u>are</u> from Ukraine.

7. Mohammed and Yuriy and Carlos are men.

Nadia <u>and</u> Jane <u>and</u> Soon <u>are</u> women.

8. I <u>is</u> a <u>mirro</u>.

I ____ from _____.

---

not

Yuriy is **not** from Mexico.
He is from Ukraine.

B. Fill in the blanks.

EXAMPLE: Mohammed <u>is</u> <u>not</u> from Ukraine.

<u>He</u> <u>is</u> from Iraq.

1. Soon <u>is</u> <u>not</u> from Mexico. <u>She</u> <u>is</u> from Korea.

2. Carlos <u>is</u> <u>not</u> a woman. <u>He</u> <u>is</u> a man.

3. Yuriy <u>and</u> Nadia <u>are</u> <u>not</u> from Iraq. <u>they</u> <u>are</u> from Ukraine.

4. Jane <u>is</u> <u>not</u> a man. <u>She</u> <u>is</u> a woman.

C. Make sentences with your partner about the students in this book and you and your classmates.

I	am					man
						men
You				a		woman
We	are					women
They		and				Mexico
						Korea
He			from			Iraq
She	is					Ukraine
It		not				

_____
_____
_____
_____
_____

D. Write these sentences with pronouns.

EXAMPLE: **Soon** is from Korea.   _She is from Korea._
▲   ▲
Name   Pronoun

1. **Jane** is from the United States.   She is from the United states.

2. **Carlos** is from Mexico.   He is from Mexico.

3. **Nadia and Yuriy** are from Ukraine.   They are from Ukraine.

4. **Mohammed** is not from Mexico.   He is not from Mexico.

5. **Soon and Carlos** are not from Iraq.   They are not from Iraq.

6. **Mohammed** is from Iraq.   He is from Iraq.

4

Contractions

I am = I'm	we are = we're
he is = he's	you are = you're
she is = she's	they are = they're
it is = it's	

is not = isn't

are not = aren't

I am not = I'm not

E. Write the sentences with contractions.

EXAMPLE: **She is** from Korea. *She's from Korea.*

1. He is from Mexico. He's from Mexico.

2. He is from Iraq. He's from Iraq.

3. They are not from Mexico. They're not from Mexico.

4. They are from Ukraine. They're from Ukraine.

5. We are men and women. We're men and women.

6. You are not from Korea. You're not from Korea.

7. I am a student. I'm a student.

8. It is a book. It's a book.

F. Write the sentences with pronouns and contractions.

EXAMPLE: **Mohammed** is a man.   *He's a man.*

1. Soon is a woman.   She's a woman.

2. Carlos is from Mexico.   He's from Mexico.

3. Nadia and Yuriy are from Ukraine.   They're from Ukraine.

4. Mohammed is from Iraq.   He's from Iraq.

5. Carlos is not from Korea.   He's not from Korea.

6. Soon and Jane are not from Mexico.   They're not from Mexico.

G. Correct these sentences.

EXAMPLE: Jane is from Ukraine.   *Jane isn't from Ukraine.*
She's from the United States.

1. Soon is a man.   Soo isn't a man.
   She's a woman.

2. Mohammed is from Korea.   Mahammed isn't from Korea.
   He's from Iraq.

3. Nadia and Yuriy are from Mexico.   Nadia and Yuriy aren't from Mexico.
   They're from Ukraine.

4. We're in Spanish class.   We're in Spanish class.
   We're in English class.

6

5. Carlos is a woman.   Carlos isn't a woman.

He's a man.

6. Nadia is from Iraq.   Nadia isn't from Iraq.

She's from Ukraine.

7. Jane and Soon are men.   Jane and Soon aren't men.

They're woman.

8. Yuriy is from Iraq.   Yuriy isn't from Iraq.

He's from Ukraine.

Yes/No Questions

Is Mohammed from Mexico?	No, he isn't.
Is Soon from Korea?	Yes, she is.
	~~Yes, she's.~~
Are Nadia and Yuriy from Ukraine?	Yes, they are.
Are Soon and Nadia men?	No, they aren't.
	~~Yes, they're~~

H. Write questions and answers. Use these words.

Is	Mohammed		a	man			No,		
	Soon			men			Yes,		
Are	Carlos	and		woman				she	is
	Nadia			women		?		he	isn't
	Jane				Mexico			they	are
	Yuriy		from		Ukraine				aren't
					Iraq				
					Korea				
					the United States				

1. Is mohamed a man? _____

2. _____ _____

3. _____ _____

4. _____ _____

5. _____ _____

6. _____ _____

7. _____ _____

8. _____ _____

9. _____ _____

I. Vowels and Consonants

Which ones are vowels? Which ones are consonants?
Write the letters in the correct column.

a b c d e f g h i j k l m n o p q r s t u v w x y z

vowels	consonants
a	b

Fred

Adele

Ray

Judy

Carl

Jane

Joey

Francine

Ronny

Charlotte

Jimmy

		husband		
		wife		
Charlotte		parents		
Jimmy		children		
Fred		father		
Adele	is	mother		
Ray	and	brother		
Jane		sister		
Carl	are	son	-in-law	
Judy	's	daughter		.
Joey		aunt	s	
Francine		uncle		
Ronny	grand	niece		
		nephew		
		cousin		

A. Look at the family. Say the names.

```
's
```

Carl is Adele**'s** son.

B. Look at the family on page 10. Write the possessive name.

EXAMPLE: Jimmy is_____*Adele's*_____grandson.

Judy is _____*Charlotte*_____ and_____*Jimmy's*_____aunt.

1. Judy is _____ sister.

2. Ray is _____ husband.

3. Adele is _____ and _____ mother.

4. Francine is _____ and _____ niece.

5. Francine and Charlotte are _____and _____ granddaughters.

6. Fred is _____ and _____ father-in-law.

7. Carl and Jane are _____ and _____ parents.

8. Joey, Francine and Ronny are _____ and _____ children.

C. Look at page 10. Answer the questions.

EXAMPLE: Is Charlotte Jimmy's sister?   _Yes, she is._

1. Is Carl Jane's husband?   _Yes, he is._

2. Are Charlotte and Jimmy Adele's children?   _No, they aren't_

3. Is Jane Ray's wife?   _No, she isn't._

4. Is Joey Judy's nephew?   _No, he isn't._

5. Is Francine Fred's grandson?   _No, she isn't._

6. Are Ronny and Joey Judy's sons?   _Yes, they are._

7. Are Ray and Judy Jimmy's parents?   _No, they aren't._

8. Is Carl Ray's brother-in-law?   _Yes, he is._

9. Is Jane Judy's sister?   _No, she is not._

10. Is Ray Charlotte's uncle?   _Yes, he is._

Who

Who is Adele's son?
Carl is.

D. Answer the questions.

EXAMPLE: Who is Carl's sister? _____Judy is._____

1. Who is Ronny's grandmother? ___Adele is_____

2. Who are Francine's cousins? ___Charlote and Jimmy are___

3. Who is Fred's wife? ___Adele is._____

4. Who is Judy's sister-in-law? ___Jane._____

5. Who is Joey's uncle? ___Carl._____

6. Who is Fred's son? ___Carl._____

7. Who are Jane's nephews? ___ey and Ronny are._____

8. Who is Ray's mother-in-law? ___Adele is._____

9. Who is Carl's father? ___Fred is._____

10. Who is Charlotte's aunt? ___Judy is._____

my   your   your   their   his   her   our

E. Write the pronoun.

EXAMPLE: Jimmy is (Charlotte's) __her__ brother.

1. Carl is (Fred and Adele's) __their__ son.

2. Jane is (Carl's) __His__ wife.

3. Joey is (Francine and Ronny's) __Their__ brother.

4. Francine is (Jane's) __her__ niece.

5. Jimmy and Charlotte are (Ronny's) __his__ cousins.

14

F. About you. Draw a picture. Complete the sentences.

1. ☐

This is my mother. ___Her___ name is ___Belem___.
      (daughter)
      (sister)

2. ☐

This is my father. ___His___ name is ___Aniceto___.
      (son)
      (brother).

3. ☐

This is me. ___My___ name is ___Catalina___.

4. ☐

This is our teacher. ___her___ name is ___Annete___.

G. Bring photographs of your family.
    Tell your classmates about them.

EXAMPLE: *This is my sister. Her name is Silvia.*
                This is my brother-in-law. His name is Steve.

H. Write sentences about the family on page 10.

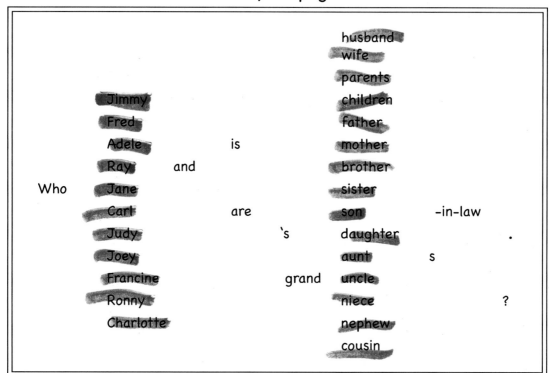

1. ___Fred is Jimmy's grandfather.___

2. ___Adele's is Ray mother-in-law.___

3. ___Ray is Judy's husband.___

4. ___Carl and Jane are Charlotte and Jimmy parents.___

5. ___Ray is Carl's brother-in-law.___

6. ___Joey, francine and Ronny are Judy's children.___

7. ___Judy and carl are fred's children.___

8. ___Fred is Judy and carl's father.___

CHAPTER 3

Students in Class

WELCOME NEW STUDENTS

Mohammed

Nadia

Soon

Carlos

Name____Mohammed Al-Tamimi____
Country ____Iraq____
Class ____Computer____
Teacher ____Mr. Rollins____

Name ____Nadia Grikova____
Country ____Ukraine____
Class ____Citizenship____
Teacher ____Mrs. Wilson____

Name____Carlos Rivas____
Country ____Mexico____
Class ____Auto Mechanics____
Teacher ____Mr. Fielding____

Name____Soon Kim____
Country ____Korea____
Class ____ESL____
Teacher ____Ms. Hawkins____

A. Look at the students in the bookstore.

Answer the questions with your partner.

EXAMPLE: Who is young?   *Mohammed is.   Mohammed and Nadia are.*

1. Who is short?

2. Who is from Ukraine?

3. Who is thin?

4. Who is in computer class?

5. Who is tall?

6. Who is heavy?

7. Who is in Mrs. Wilson's class?

8. Who is middle-aged?

9. Who is from Mexico?

10. Who is in ESL class?

Say these words with your teacher:

nombre (handwritten, left margin)

mujers (handwritten, left margin)

- Mr. —*casada*
- Mrs. —*casada*
- Miss —*joven*
- Ms. —*no estacada*

---

or

Is Carlos from Mexico?	Yes, he is.
Is Carlos in ESL **or** auto mechanics?	Auto mechanics.
Is Carlos **or** Mohammed from Iraq?	Mohammed.

B. Answer the questions.

1. Is Mohammed tall or short? _He is Tall_

2. Is Soon tall? _No, she's not._

3. Is Soon short? _Yes, she is._

4. Is Nadia young? _Yes, she is._

5. Is Nadia heavy? _No, she's not._

6. Is Soon heavy or thin? _She is Heavy_

7. Is Mohammed middle-aged? _No, he's not._

8. Is Carlos from Korea? _No, he's not._

9. Is Nadia in ESL or citizenship? _She's in Citizenship_

10. Is Carlos in auto mechanics? _Yes, he is._

Where, What

Where is Nadia from?   **Ukraine.**

What class is Soon in?   **ESL.**

C. Fill in each blank with the correct word.

que   *Donde*   *quien*

What   **Where**   **Who**

1. _Where_ is Carlos from?   Mexico.

2. _Who_ is his teacher?   Mr. Fielding.

3. _What_ class is he in?   Auto mechanics.

4. _Where_ is Nadia from?   Ukraine.

5. _What_ class is she in?   Citizenship.

6. _Who_ is her teacher?   Mrs. Wilson.

7. _Where_ is Soon from?   Korea.

8. _Who_ is her teacher?   Ms. Hawkins.

9. _Where_ is Mohammed from?   Iraq.

10. _Who_ is his teacher?   Mr. Rollins.

D. Read the story and answer the questions.

Carlos Rivas and Mohammed Al-Tamimi are new students. Carlos is from Mexico and Mohammed is from Iraq. Carlos is middle-aged and married and he has three children. He is in auto mechanics and his teacher is Mr. Fielding.

Mohammed is not married. He's single. He's tall and thin and he's 26 years old. He is in computer class and his teacher is Mr. Rollins.

1. Where is Mohammed from? _____ Iraq _____

2. Is he a new student? _____ Yes, he is. _____

3. Is he old or young? _____ Young _____

4. Is he married? _____ No, he's not. _____

5. Who is his teacher? _____ Mr. Rollins. _____

6. Who is from Mexico? _____ Carlos _____

7. Who is in computer class? _____ Mohammed _____

8. What class is Carlos in? _____ Auto Mechanics _____

9. Is Mr. Rollins his teacher? _____ No, he's not. _____

10. Is Mohammed tall or short? _____ Tall _____

E.

How many syllables are there? Where is the stress?

Listen to your teacher. Say the words.
Number the syllables. Underline the stress.

EXAMPLE: Ukraine   U <u>Kraine</u>
                             1   2

1. Korea   2. telephone   3. single   4. country

5. married   6. computer   7. citizenship   8. mechanics

F. Write sentences about the students. Use these words.

	Mohammed				Iraq
					Ukraine
					Mexico
	Nadia	is			Korea
				from	computer class .
where					ESL
		are		in	auto mechanics
what	Carlos				citizenship class
					Mr. Rollins
who			not		Mrs. Wilson
	Soon				Mr. Fielding
		and			Ms. Hawkins
	teacher				?
		or			heavy
	class				thin
					single
	he		's		married
					young
	she				middle-aged
					tall
					short

1. Where is Mohamed from?

2. Who is married?

3. _____

4. _____

5. _____

6. _____

7. _____

8. _____

a <u>l</u>emon

"l" is a consonant. See page 9.

Counting Nouns
Singular = 1   Plural = 2+

 an <u>a</u>pple

"a" is a vowel. See page 9.

 <u>an</u> apple

 apple<u>s</u>

 <u>a</u> strawberry

 strawberr<u>ies</u>

consonant + y ⟶y ies

 <u>a</u> pea<u>ch</u>

 peach<u>es</u>

sh, ch, s, x ⟶es

 <u>a</u> toma<u>to</u>

 tomato<u>es</u>

consonant + o ⟶es

(sometimes)

 <u>a</u> lea<u>f</u>

 lea<u>ves</u>

f, fe ⟶ f, fe ves

(usually)

Irregular Plurals

1 man, 2 men	1 woman, 2 women	1 fish, 2 fish	1 tooth, 2 teeth
1 person, 2 people	1 child, 2 children	1 foot, 2 feet	1 mouse, 2 mice

A. Write the singular or plural.

banana   onion   orange   potato   pear   carrot   cherry

an onion

bananas

an orange

Potatoes

cherries

Pear

Carrots

B. Write these words in the plural.

1. key _Keys_

2. dress _dresses_

3. day _days_

4. foot _feet_

5. tax _taxes_

6. clock _clocks_

7. match _matches_ _cerillos_

8. library _libraries_

9. housewife _hosewives_

10. family _families_

11. church _churches_

12. tomato _tomatoes_

C.

How many **syllables** are there? Where is the **stress**?
Listen to your teacher. Say the words. Number the syllables. Underline the stress.

1. carrot   2. peaches   3. lemon   4. strawberry   5. potato

6. pear   7. apple   8. banana   9. onion   10. children

foil
apples
bananas
bread
butter
carrots
cereal
a chicken
eggs
flour
ice cream
a lemon
lettuce
milk
mustard
oil
onions
potatoes
rice
soda
soup
cookies

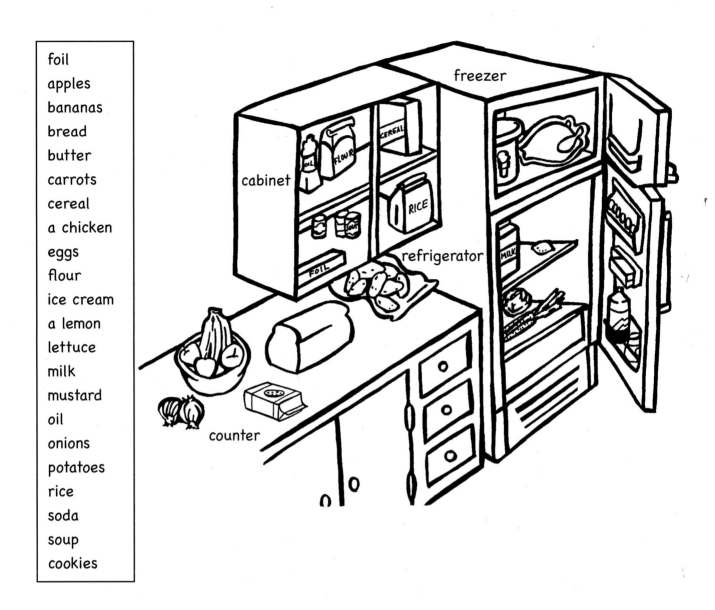

D. Write the names of the food in the correct columns.

Singular (a , an)	Plural (s)	Non-count (no a, no an, no s)
a chicken	*apples*	*foil*
milk		bread
foil		butter
~~bread~~		
~~butter~~		
cereal		
flour		
Ice cream		
a lemon		
lettuce		
oil		

24

The food in the non-count column comes in <u>containers</u>.

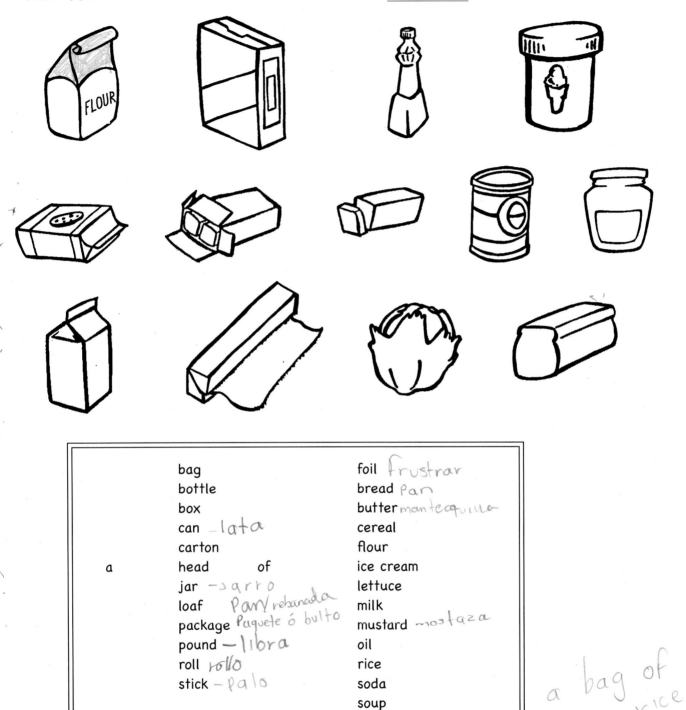

	bag	foil _frustrar_
	bottle	bread _pan_
	box	butter _mantecaquilla_
	can _-lata_	cereal
	carton	flour
a	head of	ice cream
	jar _-jarro_	lettuce
	loaf _Pan/rebanada_	milk
	package _Paquete ó bulto_	mustard _-mostaza_
	pound _-libra_	oil
	roll _rollo_	rice
	stick _-palo_	soda
		soup
		cookies

a bag of rice

E. Talk about the food in the kitchen with your partner.

EXAMPLE: _a loaf of bread_____

You cannot count non-count nouns.

2 mus~~tards~~

You can count containers.

2 ja**r**s of mustard

F. Count the containers of food.

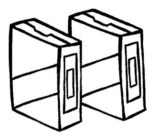

a can of soup
_____

2 box of Carton
_____

3 heads of lettuce
_____

a box of cookies
_____

a bag of flour
_____

2 leaves of bread
_____

3 bottes of oil
_____

2 Jars of Ice Cream
_____

G. What's in the kitchen? Look at page 24.

1. _____a bag of rice_____
2. _____a box of cereal_____
3. _____a bunch of bananas_____
4. _____a carton of milk_____
5. _____a bag of flour_____
6. _____a botte of soup_____
7. _____a lemon_____
8. _____a chiken_____
9. _____two onions_____
10. _____three carrots_____
11. _____

11. _____a carton of ice cream_____
12. _____a butter of oil_____
13. _____a carton of eggs_____
14. _____a Package of cookies_____
15. _____a loaf of bread_____
16. _____a butter of soda_____
17. _____
18. _____
19. _____
20. _____
21. _____

Some, There is, There are

If you don't know the exact amount, you can also use "some" with <u>plural count nouns</u> and <u>non-count nouns</u>. Use "are" with <u>plural</u> and "is" with <u>non-count</u>.

EXAMPLES: There <u>are</u> **some** apple<u>s</u> on the counter.

There<u>'s</u> **some** flour in the cabinet.

You <u>cannot</u> use "some" with singular count nouns because a/an = one.

There's so̶m̶e **a** lemon in the refrigerator.

You <u>cannot</u> use "some" with one container.

There's so̶m̶e **a** box of cereal in the cabinet.

There are **some** can**s** of soup in the cabinet.

H. Read the question and circle the correct answer.

1. Is there a box of cereal in the refrigerator?   Yes, there is.   (No, there isn't.)

2. Is there a bag of rice in the cabinet?   Yes, there is.   No, there isn't.

3. Are there seven apples on the counter?   Yes, there are.   No, there aren't.

4. Is there some bread on the counter?   Yes, there is   No, there isn't.

5. Are there 3 boxes of cookies in the cabinet?   Yes, there are.   No, there aren't.

6. Is there a peach in the refrigerator?   Yes, there is.   No, there isn't.

7. Are there some potatoes on the counter?   Yes, there are.   No, there aren't.

8. Is there a lemon in the refrigerator?   Yes, there is.   No, there isn't.

9. Is there a chicken in the freezer?   Yes, there is.   No, there isn't.

10. Are there 5 oranges on the counter?   Yes, there are.   No, there aren't.

I. Complete the sentences with "There is" or "There are".

1. _____There is_____ a bag of flour in the cabinet.

2. _____ a jar of mustard in the refrigerator.

3. _____ three cans of soup in the cabinet.

4. _____ some eggs in the refrigerator.

5. _____ a bottle of oil in the cabinet.

6. _____ a carton of ice cream in the freezer.

7. _____ some rice in the cabinet.

8. _____ a loaf of bread on the counter.

9. _____ a pound of butter in the refrigerator.

10. _____ a box of cereal in the cabinet.

J. Look at page 24. Write sentences about the kitchen with these words.

There	is	a	box		of	soup		the
			carton			eggs		
						foil		
						apples		
	are	2	bottle	s		bread		
			jar			rice		
		3	bag			milk	in	
			can	es		ice cream		
		6	loaf			mustard	on	
			pound			cereal		
			package			oil		
			roll			chicken		.
			head			bananas		
						lemon		
						onions		
						potatoes	freezer	
						butter		
						cookies	refrigerator	
						carrots		
			some			flour	cabinet	
						soda		
						lettuce	counter	

1. _____

2. _____

3. _____

4. _____

5. _____

6. _____

7. _____

8. _____

9. _____

K. Look in <u>your</u> kitchen. Write eight sentences about the food in your kitchen.

EXAMPLE: *There's a bag of rice in my cabinet.*
_____

1. _____

2. _____

3. _____

4. _____

5. _____

6. _____

7. _____

8. _____

L. Talk together in a group.

Ask and answer questions about the food in your kitchen.

EXAMPLE: **A.** *What's in your kitchen?* **B.** *There are 3 cans of tuna in my kitchen.*

A. *There are 3 cans of tuna in Kim's kitchen.*

M.

> How many **syllables** are there? Where is the **stress**?

Listen to your teacher. Say the words.
Number the syllables.   Underline the stress.

1. cereal

2. cookies

3. carton

4. lettuce

5. package

6. butter

7. refrigerator

8. bread

9. freezer

N.

This, That, These, Those

When one thing is near you, use "this".
When one thing is not near you, use "that".
When two or more things are near you, use "these".
When two or more things are not near you, use "those".

This is a jar.

That is a bottle.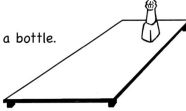

These are apples.

Those are bananas.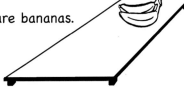

N. Write this, that, these or those.

1. _____ is a _____.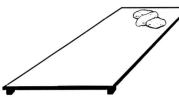

2. _____ are _____.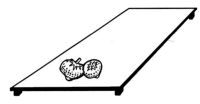

3. _____ are _____.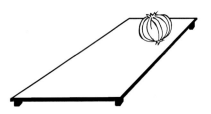

4. _____ is an _____.

Measurement containers

gallon

half gallon

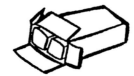
pound

stick

4 ounces

half gallon

quart

pint

half pint

cup
(8 ounces)

O. Write sentences about the measurements.

There		a	half pint	s	in	a	half pint
	is	2	pint				pint
	are	4	quart				quart
		8	half gallon				half gallon
		16	gallon				gallon
		32	cup				cup
		64	ounce				pound .
		128	half pound				
			pound				
			stick				

1. _____*There are 4 quarts in a gallon.*_____

2. _____

3. _____

4. _____

5. _____

6. _____

32

CHAPTER 5

Where is it?

A. Write the preposition in the sentence.

on   under   next to   between   behind   in   over   in front of
(in back of)   (above)

1. The milk is ___In from of___ the bag.

behind

2. The milk is ___in back of___ the bag.

3. The milk is ___between___ the bags.

4. The milk is ___in___ the bag.

5. The milk is ___nex to___ the bag.

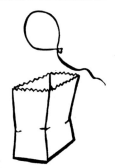

6. The balloon is ___over___ the bag.

7. The milk is ___on___ the table.

8. The milk is ___under___ the table.

B. Write the name on the room.

        living room   **bedroom**   **kitchen**   **bathroom**

C. Talk and write about the people in the house.

        EXAMPLE: *Charlotte is in the kitchen.*

1. Jimmy and Jane are in the bathroom

2. Carl is in the bedroom

3. Charlotte is in the kitchen

4. _____

5. _____

34

D. Write the name under the picture.

1.

dresser

2.

bookcase

3.

Mirror

4.
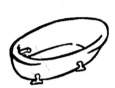
bathtub

5.

armchair

6.
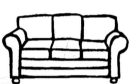
sofa

7.

bed

8.

refrigerator

9.

night table

10.

sink

11.

coffee table

12.

toile

13.

medicine cabinet

14.

Dining table

15.

stove

E. Look at the house on page 34. Write the preposition.

on   under   next to   between   behind   in   over   in front of

EXAMPLE: The end table is ___*next to*___ the sofa.

1. The sofa is ___in___ the living room.

2. The lamp is ___on___ the night table.

3. The sink is ___between___ the refrigerator and the stove.

4. The rug is ___in from of___ the bathtub.

5. The television is ___under___ the picture.

6. The bookcase is ___nex to___ the night table.

7. The mirror is ___over___ the sink.

8. Fred is ___in from of___ the sofa.

F. Look at the house on page 34. Read the sentence and circle yes or no.

1. The television is in the bedroom.   yes   (no)

2. The stove is next to the sink.   (yes)   no

3. The sink is under the mirror.   (yes)   no

4. The picture is over the sofa.   yes   (no)

5. The bookcase is in the living room.   yes   (no)

6. The night table is between the bookcase and the bed.   (yes)   no

7. The rug is behind the bathtub.   yes   (no)

8. The end table is on the lamp.   yes   (no)

36

G. Look at the house on page 34. Ask and answer questions with your partner.

EXAMPLE: *Where is the bed?*   *It's next to the night table.*

Where are the towels?   *They're in the closet.*

H. Write answers to the questions.

1. Where's the refrigerator? It's nex to the window.

2. Where's the toilet? It's nex to the sink.

3. Where's the dresser? It's under the window

4. Where's the night table? It's between the bookcase and the bed

5. Where's the mirror? It's above the sink.

6. Where are the books? They are in the bookcase.

7. Where is the picture? It's above the tv.

8. Where is the television? It's in from of the sofa.

9. Where is the kitchen sink? It's under the window.

10. Where is Charlotte? She's in the kitchen.

11. Where is Carl? He's in the bedroom.

12. Where is the plant? It's in the living room.

13. Where are Fred and Adele? They're in the living room.

14. Where are the lamps? They're in the living room and the bedroom.

the	clock		on		cabinets	
	plant		under		dishwasher	
	sauce pan	is	in		stove	
	toaster		next to		refrigerator	
	microwave	are	between	the	window	.
	curtains		over		sink	
	paper towels		behind		counter	
	telephone		in front of		window sill	
	trash can				wall	
	calendar					
	frying pans					
	tea kettle					

I. Write 10 sentences about the kitchen. Use the words in the box.
   Try to use all of the prepositions.

1. _____

2. _____

3. _____

4. _____

5. _____

6. _____

7. _____

8. _____

9. _____

10. _____

J.

How many syllables are there? Where is the stress?

Listen to your teacher. Say the words.
Number the syllables. Underline the stress.

1. between   3. medicine   5. over   7. calendar

2. kitchen   4. stove   6. toilet   8. dishwasher

CHAPTER 6

In the Community

A. Read the words. Write the name under the picture.

bank	hospital	fire station	drugstore	school	video store
dentist	laundromat	library	restaurant	supermarket	barber shop
movie theater		post office	service station	police station	

1.

bank

2.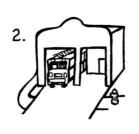

Fire station

3.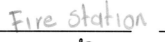

drugstore

4.

restaurant

5.

Police station

6.

Post office

7.

dentist

8.

barber shop

9.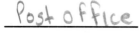

Movie theater

10.

laundromat

11.

School

12.

Supermarket

13.

Service station
gas.

14.

Video store

15.

library

16.

Hospital

Main St.

on

The hospital is **on** Main Street.

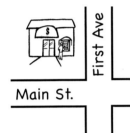

First Ave

Main St.

on the corner of

The bank is **on the corner of** Main St. and First Ave.

around the corner from

The laundromat **is around the corner from** the dentist.

First Ave

VIDEO

Main St.

across from

The video store is **across from** the school.

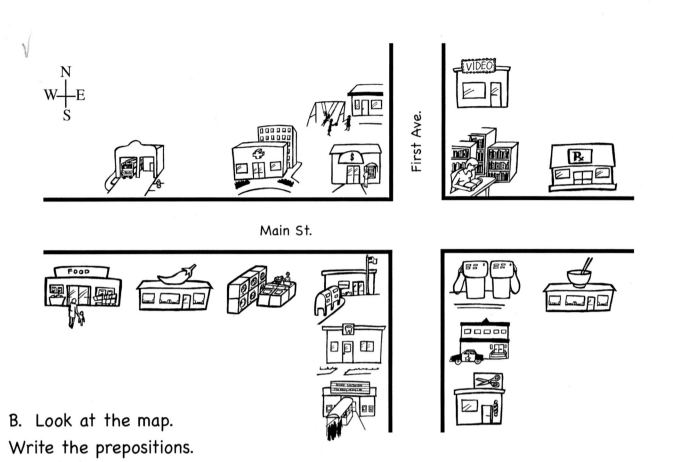

First Ave.

Main St.

B. Look at the map.
Write the prepositions.

on   on the corner of   between   next to   across from   around the corner from

1. The fire station is ___between___ Main Street.

2. The library is _____Main Street and First Avenue.

3. The drugstore is ___across from___ the Chinese restaurant.

4. The dentist is ___between___ the post office and the movie theater.

5. The video store is ___around the corner from___ the drugstore.

6. The supermarket is ___Nex to___ the Mexican restaurant.

7. The laundromat is ___on___ Main St. ___across from___ the hospital.

8. The police station is ___on___ First Ave. ___around the corner from___ the Chinese restaurant.

9. The bank is ___on___ Main St. and First Ave., ___nex to___ the school.

10. The laundromat is ___between___ the Mexican restaurant and the post office,

_____ the hospital.

C. Look at the map on page 42. Ask and answer questions with your partner.

> EXAMPLE: *Where is the Chinese restaurant?*
>
> *It's on Main St., across from the drugstore.*

D. Look at the map. Answer the questions with your partner.

1. What's on the northeast corner of Main St. and First Ave.? library is.

2. Is the school on Main St.? NO, it isn't

3. Where is the police station? Is between the gas

4. What's across from the video store?

5. Is the laundromat next to the Mexican restaurant or the Chinese restaurant?

6. What's around the corner from the hospital?

7. Where is the bank?

8. Is the dentist across from the police station?

9. Is the barber shop on First Ave. or Main St.?

10. Where is the fire station?

E.

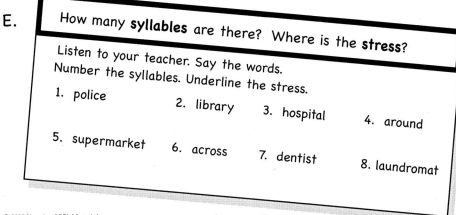

How many **syllables** are there? Where is the **stress**?

Listen to your teacher. Say the words.
Number the syllables. Underline the stress.

1. police   2. library   3. hospital   4. around

5. supermarket   6. across   7. dentist   8. laundromat

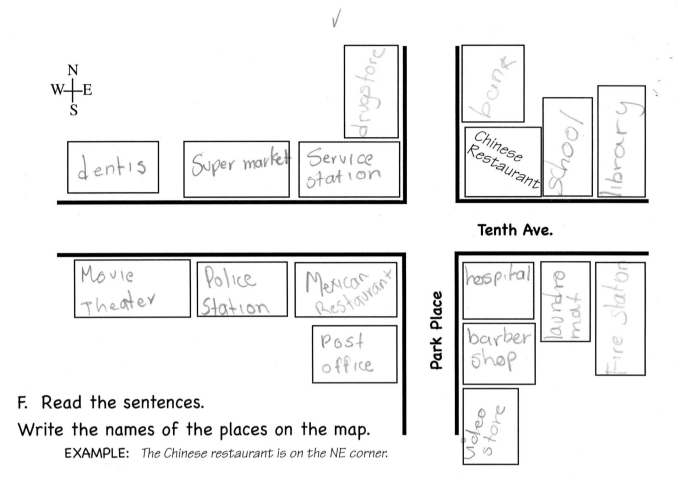

Tenth Ave.

Park Place

F. Read the sentences.

Write the names of the places on the map.

EXAMPLE: *The Chinese restaurant is on the NE corner.*

1. The bank is next to the restaurant on Park Place.

2. The drugstore is across from the bank.

3. The school is around the corner from the bank.

4. The school is between the Chinese restaurant and the library.

5. The fire station is across from the library.

6. The laundromat is between the fire station and the hospital.

7. The Mexican restaurant is on the SW corner.

8. The service station is on the last corner.

9. The supermarket is between the service station and the dentist on 10th Ave.

10. The barber shop is around the corner from the laudromat on Park Place.

11. The post office is across from the barber shop.

12. The video store is next to the barber shop.

13. The police station is around the corner from the post office on 10th Ave.

14. The movie theater is across from the dentist.

G. Look at the map on page 44. Answer the questions with your partner.

1. Where is the bank?

2. Is the barber shop on Park Pl. or 10th Ave.?

3. Is the supermarket across from the police station?

4. What's around the corner from the laundromat?

5. What's between the video store and the hospital?

6. Where is the service station?

7. Is the hospital on the SW corner or the SE corner?

8. Where is the post office?

9. What's next to the fire station?

10. What's across from the drugstore?

H. Think about <u>your</u> town or neighborhood here in North America.

1. Where is the post office? _____

2. Where is the police station? _____

3. Where is the high school?_____

4. Where is the library? _____

5. Where is the hospital? _____

6. Where is the fire station? _____

I. Write sentences about the map.

N
W —|— E
S

NW

NE

Summer Ave.

Spring St.

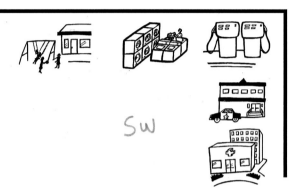

SW

SE

The	fire station	is	on		
	hospital	are	next to		
	bank		between		
	school		across from		
	video store				Spring Street
	library	and			Summer Avenue
	drugstore				
	police station		on the	SW corner of	
	supermarket		" "	NW " "	
	Mexican restaurant		" "	NE " "	
	laundromat		" "	SE " "	
	Chinese restaurant				
	post office				
	dentist				
	barber shop		around the corner from		
	service station				

1. _____

2. _____

3. _____

4. _____

5. _____

6. _____

7. _____

In a Restaurant

A. Look at the picture. Answer the questions with your partner.

1. Who is eating a hamburger?
   Marla is

2. Who is waiting in line?
   Nadia is

3. Who is cleaning tables?
   Cathy is

4. Who is drinking a soda?
   Vicky is

5. Who is paying for dinner?
   Yuriy is

6. Who is getting a napkin?
   Soon is

7. Who is putting trash in the trash can?
   Carlos is

8. Who is getting ketchup?
   Jane

Present Continuous

We use the present continuous to talk about <u>NOW</u>.

| I | am |
| | am not |

he / she / it	is	+	verb + ing
	isn't		
we / you / they	are		
	aren't		

Present Continuous Spelling

1. 1 consonant + e = X̶ + ing

    EXAMPLE: smile — smiling

2. 1 vowel + 1 consonant = 2 consonants + ing (except x, y, w)

    EXAMPLE: sit — sitting

                sew — sewing

B. Write the -ing forms for the following verbs:

1. run ning

2. rain ning

3. sleep ing

4. write writing

5. cry cring

6. erase _____

7. fix Fixing

8. live living

9. cut cutting

10. dance dancing

11. put Putting

12. smoke smoking

13. study studying

14. snow snowing

15. say saying

16. take taking

17. get getting

18. walk walking

19. ride riding

20. speak speaking

21. stand standing

48

C. Look at the picture on page 47.
   Complete the sentences with the right verbs. Use the present continuous.

hold	get	put	wait	give
clean	eat	drink	pay	stand

1. Carlos __is putting__ his trash in the trash can.

2. Yuriy __is paying__ for lunch.

3. Curtis __is giving__ Yuriy his change.

4. Cathy __is cleaning__ tables.

5. Soon __is holding__ a soda.

6. Nadia __is waiting__ in line.

7. Vicky __is drinking__ a soda.

8. Soon __is getting__ a napkin.

9. Marla and Vicky __are eating__ dinner.

10. Carlos __is standing__ behind Jane.

Present Continuous yes/no questions

Is Curtis working?   Yes, he is.
Is Soon sitting?   No, she isn't.
Are Jane and Carlos standing?   Yes, they are.
Are Nadia and Yuriy eating?   No, they aren't.

D. Look at the picture on page 47. Answer the questions.

   EXAMPLE: Is Cathy cleaning tables? __Yes, she is.__

1. Is Vicky drinking a soda? __Yes, she is.__

2. Is Jane drinking a soda? __No, she isn't.__

3. Are Yuriy and Nadia eating breakfast? __No, they aren't.__

4. Is Marla giving change? __No, she isn't.__

5. Is Jane getting salt and pepper? __No, she isn't.__

6. Is Cathy cleaning the floor? __No, she isn't.__

7. Is Carlos eating? __No, he isn't.__

8. Is Soon holding a soda? __Yes, she is.__

E. Put the words in the correct order.

EXAMPLE: Yuriy / dinner / paying / Curtis / is / . / for / his
Yuriy is paying Curtis for his dinner.

1. hamburger / Marla / Vicky / eating / . / talking / is / to / and / a

   Marla is eating a hamburger and talking to vicky.

2. the / washing / . / Cathy / kitchen / isn't / dishes / in

   Cathy isn't washing dishes in the kitchen

3. standing / of / Jane / Carlos / in / . / is / front

   Jane is standing in from of carlos

4. dinner / is / Mohammed / picking / . / up / his

   Mohamed is Picking up his dinner.

5. and / Soon / ? / Jane / sitting / Are / a / at / table

   Are soon and Jane sitting at a table

6. ketchup / getting / Soon / ? / Is / napkins / or

   _____

7. change / Curtis / . / giving / Yuriy / is / his

   _____

50

F. Write sentences about the picture on page 47.

Mohammed			talk				the	trash can	
Yuriy			pick up					counter	
Nadia	and		put					dinner	
Carlos	or		clean				a	coffee	
Jane			drink					soda	.
Soon		is	get				his	trash	
Vicky			eat	-ing	at			hamburger	
Marla		are	work		in			ketchup	
Cathy			stand		next to			table	?
Curtis			sit		behind			change	
			pay for		in front of			cash register	,
he		not	wait		across from			line	Yes
she			give		to			napkins	No
they			hold		for				

1. Cathy is cleaning a table.

2. Vicky is drinking a soda.

3. Soon is getting napkins.

4. Mohamed is Pick up the dinner

5. Carlos is Putting trash in the trash can.

6. Jane is getting Ketchup.

7. _____

8. _____

9. _____

10. _____

G. Read the story. Then read each sentence.
Circle "Yes" if the sentence is true. Circle "No" if the sentence is false.

Before Class

It's almost class time. Our friends are not at work now. They're hungry and they're having dinner. Mohammed is picking up his food. His dinner is on a tray. Yuriy and Nadia are paying Curtis. Jane is getting some ketchup for her hamburger and Soon is getting napkins. Carlos is finished. He's putting his trash in the trash can. Cathy and Curtis are students too. Their classes are in the morning, but they are working now. They work from 4:00 to 9:00. Everybody is busy!

1.	Soon is at work.	Yes	(No)
2.	It's lunch time.	Yes	(No)
3.	The cashier is giving Yuriy change.	(Yes)	No
4.	Vicki is sitting next to Marla.	Yes	(No)
5.	Cathy is a student.	(Yes)	No
6.	Jane is eating Mexican food for dinner.	Yes	(No)
7.	Curtis is cleaning tables.	Yes	(No)
8.	Mohammed is getting french fries for dinner.	(Yes)	No
9.	Vicky is drinking coffee with her dinner.	Yes	(No)
10.	Carlos is standing in front of Jane.	Yes	(No)

H. Fill in the blanks with the correct words:

Who   **What**   **Where**

1. _Who_ is getting napkins?   Soon is.
2. _What_ is Cathy doing?   Cleaning tables.
3. _Where_ is Curtis working?   Behind the counter.
4. _What_ is Curtis giving Yuriy?   His change.
5. _Who_ is Marla talking to?   Vicky.
6. _who_ is sitting across from Vicky?   Marla is.
7. _Where_ is Jane standing?   In front of Carlos.
8. _what_ is Vicky drinking?   A soda.
9. _What_ is Yuriy doing?   Getting his change.
10. _who_ is getting ketchup?   Jane is.
11. _where_ is Mohammed standing?   At the counter.
12. _what_ is Mohammed doing?   Picking up his food.

52

do	
What is Jane **doing**?	Getting ketchup.
What is Jane **getting?**	Ketchup.

You cannot say "What is Cathy <u>working</u>?"
You say "What is Cathy **doing**?"

I. Circle the correct answer.

EXAMPLE:

What is Jane doing?   (a. Getting ketchup.)   b. Ketchup.
What is Jane getting?   a. Getting ketchup.   (b. Ketchup.)

1. What is Marla doing?   (a. Eating a hamburger.)   b. A hamburger.

2. What is Marla eating?   a. Eating a hamburger.   (b. A hamburger.)

3. What is Yuriy doing?   (a. Getting his change.)   b. His change.

4. What is Yuriy getting?   a. Getting his change.   (b. His change.)

5. What is Mohammed doing?   (a. Picking up his food.)   b. His food.

6. What is Mohammed picking up?   a. Picking up his food.   (b. His food.)

7. What is Cathy cleaning?   a. Cleaning tables.   (b. Tables.)

8. What is Cathy doing?   (a. Cleaning tables.)   b. Tables.

9. What is Vicky drinking?   a. Drinking a soda.   (b. A soda.)

10. What is Vicky doing?   (a. Drinking a soda.)   b. A soda.

J. Write the words in the questions in the correct order.
Answer the questions.

EXAMPLE: Curtis / What / ? / doing / is   *What is Curtis doing?*   *Giving Yuriy change.*

1. drinking / Vicky / ? / What / is
   What is Vicky drinking?   a soda.

2. trash/ ? / Who / in / is / putting / the / trash can
   Who is putting trash in the trash can? Carlos is.

3. What / Mohammed / ? / picking / is / up
   What is mohammed picking up?   his food.

4. is / Carlos / ? / Where / standing
   Where is carlos standing?   behind the jane

5. Cathy / What / is / ? / doing
   what is cathy doing?   a cleaning tables.

6. cashier / ? / is / Where / standing / the
   where is standing the cashier? behind the counter.

7. change / Yuriy / Who / ? / is / giving
   Who is giving change Yuny?   Curtis is.

8. ? / Marla / Where / sitting / is
   Where is sitting Marla?   across from vicky

9. Yuriy / standing / ? / is / next to / Who
   Who is standing nex to yuriy? Mohammed is

10. Marla / talking / ? / Who /to / is
    Who is talking to Marla?   Vicky is

K. Write questions and answers about the picture on page 47.

Who	Mohammed		talk				the	counter		
	Curtis		hold					dinner		
	Yuriy	and	put					coffee		
	Nadia		clean			a		soda	s	.
What	Marla		drink					ketchup		
	Vicky	is	get			his		hamburgers		
Where	Carlos		eat	-ing	in			napkin		
	Jane	are	work		for			table		?
	Soon		stand		next to			change		
	Cathy		sit		behind			cash register		
		not	pay		in front of			french fries		
			look		across from			trash		
			give		at			trash can		
			wait		to					
			do							

1. _____

2. _____

3. _____

4. _____

5. _____

6. _____

7. _____

8. _____

9. _____

10. _____

L. Talk with a partner. Ask and answer these questions.

He is cashier

1. What is Curtis doing?

2. What is Jane getting?

3. Who is standing behind Yuriy?

4. What is Soon holding?

5. Where is Carlos putting his trash?

6. Who is sitting across from Vicky?

7. Is it lunch time?   *No, it isn't*

8. What is Mohammed doing?
   He, is Pick up. a food

9. What is Yuriy doing?
   He, is Paying the cashier.

10. Who is sitting at a table?
    Vicky is

11. Who is working?
    Cathy is

12. What is Soon doing?
    She is gettin a napkin.

M. Look at your class. Ask and answer questions with your partner.

EXAMPLES: Where is the teacher standing?   What am I doing?

Who is smiling?   What are you doing?

What is the teacher doing?   Am I speaking French?

Are you sitting next to _____?   Who is speaking _____?

N.

> ## How many **syllables** are there? Where is the **stress**?
>
> Listen to your teacher. Say the words.
> Number the syllables. Underline the stress.
>
> 1. hamburger   2. counter   3. cash register
>
> 4. ketchup   5. everybody   6. cleaning

CHAPTER 8

Talking About Things

A. What is it?

_____   _____   _____

_____   _____

B. Draw a line.

a dime	25¢
a penny	50¢
a half dollar	5¢
a nickel	1¢
a quarter	10¢

Pronouns for things	
a dime =	**it**
2 dimes =	**them**

you

me   you   him   her   them

us   it   them

C. Watch two or three students practice with money in front of the class.
They will use the words in the box.

EXAMPLE: *Please take a penny and give it to her.*
Please take 2 quarters and keep them.

please	take	a	penny		me
			nickel		
	give	2	dime	-s	her
			quarter		us
	keep	3		to	him
and			it		them
			them		

take   give   keep

D. Sit in a group of 4 or 5 students.

Take the coins from your pocket or purse, or use the coins your teacher
gives you. (Remember how much!)

Look at the coins.
What's the name of each one?
How much is it?

Put the coins together in the middle of your group.
Choose a classmate from your group.
Tell your classmate what to do.

EXAMPLE: *Please, take a nickel. Give <u>it</u> to <u>me</u>.*

Please, take 2 dimes. Give <u>them</u> to <u>her</u>.

Please, take a quarter. Keep <u>it</u>.

E. Complete the sentences with the object pronoun.

me   him   her   us   them   it

1. Take 2 nickels. Give _____ to me.

2. Take a dime. Give _____ to him.

3. Take 3 pennies. Keep _____.

F. Put the words in the correct order.

1. give / and / 2 / me / them / Take / . / to / pennies

_____

2. dime / keep / Take / . / a / it / and

_____

3. them / and / us / a / nickels / Take / . / 4 / and / quarter / give / to

_____

4. a / half dollar / give / to / . / Take / and / it / her

_____

5. give / her / dimes / Take / . / 2 / and / him / to / to / and / 1 / 1

_____

G. Look at the picture of the restaurant on page 47.
   Write the correct object pronoun in each sentence.

   me   her   him   it   us   them

1. Yuriy is saying, "Please give_____the change."

2. Is Nadia standing behind Mohammed and Yuriy? Yes, she's standing behind _____.

3. Yuriy is talking to Curtis. He's looking at _____.

4. Is Soon holding a soda? Yes, she's holding _____.

5. Yuriy and Nadia are together. He tells Nadia, "Please get _____ a table."

6. Is Nadia taking the change? No, she isn't taking _____.

7. Is Soon taking 2 napkins? Yes, she's taking _____.

8. Is Carlos looking at Mohammed? No, he isn't looking at _____.

9. Is Curtis talking to Soon? No, he isn't talking to _____.

10. Is Cathy cleaning a table? Yes, she's cleaning _____.

60

CHAPTER 9

Occupations

A. Read the words. Write the names of the occupations under the pictures.

bus driver
painter
carpenter
house keeper
housewife
child care worker
cashier
mail carrier
teacher
plumber

1.

_____

2.

_____

3.

_____

4.

_____

5.

_____

6.

_____

7.

_____

8.

_____

9.

_____

10.

_____

B. Write the names under the pictures.

1.

_____

2.

_____

3.

_____

4.

_____

5.

_____

Nadia is a nurse.

Carlos is a mechanic.

Yuriy and Soon are factory workers.

Jane is a housewife.

Mohammed is an accountant.

<table>
<tr><td>**can**</td><td></td></tr>
</table>

I
you
he   **can** +   verb (**no S no ing**)
she
we
they

EXAMPLE:

I can speak English.

I can speak̶s̶ English.

I can speak̶i̶n̶g̶ English.

C. Nadia is a nurse.

She **can** take your temperature.

She can give shots.

She can change a bandage.

She can give a bedbath.

She can _____

She can _____

Carlos is a mechanic.

He **can** _____

He can _____

He can _____

He can _____

I am a / an _____ .

I **can** _____

I can _____

I can _____

D. Talk to your classmates.

What is your job?   *I'm a / an* _____.

What can you do?   *I can* _____.

Write 3 names and occupations here. What can your classmates do?

1. _____ is _____.

    He/She can _____.

2. _____ is _____.

    He/She can _____.

3. _____ is _____.

    He/She can _____.

E. Look at page 62 and think about the students in this book and think about your classmates.

Make sentences using these words and words you add about your classmates.

Nadia			nurse		fix pipes
Carlos		a	mechanic		paint walls
Mohammed	is		housekeeper		give shots
Yuriy		an	cashier		make budgets
Jane			factory worker		make furniture .
Soon	and		painter		teach children
I			accountant	s	fix cars
	are		teacher		make change
_____			housewife		cook
_____		not	plumber		vacuum
_____			carpenter		
_____	am		_____		_____
he			_____		_____
she	can		_____		_____
they			_____		_____

EXAMPLE: _Carlos is a mechanic. He can fix cars._

1. _____

2. _____

3. _____

4. _____

5. _____

6. _____

7. _____

8. _____

9. _____

10. _____

F.

How many **syllables** are there? Where is the **stress**?

Listen to your teacher. Say the words.
Number the syllables. Underline the stress.

1. teacher   2. plumber   3. carpenter   4. nurse

5. mechanic   6. cashier   7. housewife   8. mail carrier

Resume

Personal Information

Name_____Telephone #_____
            first   last

Address _____ Email _____
          number   street   apt

               _____ Fax _____
            city   state   zip

Education

School	City/Country	Degree	Year
_____	_____	_____	_____
_____	_____	_____	_____
_____	_____	_____	_____

Skills

I can _____

I can _____

Experience

Dates from/to	Job	Company
_____	_____	_____
_____	_____	_____
_____	_____	_____

References

Name	Title	Company	Telephone Fax or Email
_____	_____	_____	_____
_____	_____	_____	_____
_____	_____	_____	_____

CHAPTER 10

At the Job Agency

Som, Habte, Hazim and Tran are looking for jobs. They're waiting for their interviews. Hazim is looking for a job as a carpenter. Tran and Habte are looking for jobs as cashiers. Som is looking for a job as a housekeeper. They're all a little nervous.

A. What do you think they can do? Talk with a partner.

			vacuum
Tran			frame a house
Habte		can	make change
Hazim	and		build cabinets
Som			put in windows .
			clean windows
			use a cash register
			dust

Asking and answering questions with can

Can Hazim build cabinets?   **Yes**, he **can**.

Can Som make change?   **No**, she **can't**.

B. Ask and answer questions with your partner. Use these words.
Think of new questions, too.

play the piano	cook	use a computer	drive
speak Russian	type	fix engines	sew
take care of children	paint	make change	vacuum

EXAMPLE: A. *Can you cook?*   B. *Yes, I can.*

B. *No, I can't.*

can   vs.   now

Som **can** clean windows, but she**'s** not clean**ing** now.
She's sitting at the Job Agency now.

You cannot use can with -ing.
Som can clean🗙 windows.

C. Think about the people on page 67. Write sentences following the example:

EXAMPLE: _Som can clean windows, but she's not cleaning now._

1. _____

2. _____

3. _____

4. _____

5. _____

6. _____

D. Answer the questions. Be careful. Some are "can"; some are "now".

EXAMPLE: Can Hazim build furniture? _____ Yes, he can. _____

Is Hazim building now? _____ No, he isn't. _____

1. Can Som vacuum? _____

2. Is Tran looking for a job? _____

3. Can Habte and Tran make change? _____

4. Can Hazim clean bathrooms? _____

5. Are Tran and Habte using a cash register? _____

6. Can Som build houses? _____

7. Can Hazim make change? _____

8. Is Som vacuuming? _____

9. Are Tran and Som sitting? _____

10. Can Som dust? _____

E. Write sentences about your life. Follow the example.

EXAMPLE: _I can swim, but I'm not swimming now._

1. _____

2. _____

3. _____

4. _____

5. _____

What kind of, Why

What kind of job is Hazim looking for? **A job as a carpenter.**
What kind of car is he driving? **A Toyota.**
Why is he holding an umbrella? **Because it's raining.**

F. Complete the sentences with one of the following words:

where   **why**   **who**   **what**   **what kind of**

1. _____ can frame a house?   Hazim can.

2. _____ is Hazim doing?   He's looking for a job.

3. _____ can Hazim do?   Build furniture and houses.

4. _____ is Hazim looking for a job?   Because he needs money.

5. _____ is Som sitting?   Across from Hazim.

6. _____ can make change?   Habte and Tran can.

70

7. _____ is Tran looking for?   A job.

8. _____ job is Tran looking for?   A job as a cashier.

9. _____ is sitting behind Hazim?   Tran is.

10. _____ can Habte use?   A cash register.

G. Look at page 67. Read the answers and write the questions.

1. _Where_ _____? At the Job Agency.

2. _Can_ _____? Yes, he can.

3. _Can_ _____? No, they can't.

4. _What kind of_ _____? A job as a housekeeper.

5. _Who_ _____? Tran can.

6. _Who_ _____? Hazim is.

7. _Who_ _____? Habte and Tran are.

8. _What_ _____? She can dust and vacuum.

9. _Can_ _____? Yes, they can.

10. _Where_ _____? Next to Som.

H. Write sentences about the picture. Use these words.

where		is	look		for	job
what kind of			sit		in	cashier
why	Habte	are	build		as	housekeeper
what	Som		vacuum	-ing	on	carpenter
who	Hazim		use		at	houses
	Tran	and	make			change s
		but	dust		a	cabinets
	he		clean		an	cash register .
	she	can	frame		the	Job Agency
	they		do			windows ?
		not	stand		now	
			put in			

1. _____

2. _____

3. _____

4. _____

5. _____

6. _____

7. _____

8. _____

9. _____

10. _____

I. Write your own employment application.

Employment Application

PERSONAL INFORMATION

Name	Social Security Number
Present Address	Telephone Number

NUMBER   STREET

CITY   STATE   ZIP CODE

EDUCATION

Names of Schools	City & Country	Month & Year From — To	Graduated ☐ yes ☐ no	Year
			☐ ☐	
			☐ ☐	
			☐ ☐	

PREVIOUS WORK EXPERIENCE Account completely for the last five years.

Name & Address of Last Employer	Dates	Kind of Business	Duties
1.	From To		
2.	From To		
3.	From To		

EMPLOYMENT DESIRED

☐ Permanent   ☐ Temporary   ☐ Part-time   ☐ Summer

Work Preferred? _____

PLEASE READ BEFORE SIGNING

I affirm that all information included on this application is true and correct. Any false information I have given can be considered sufficient cause for discharge. I authorize all former employers to answer questions in reference to this application.

Signature _____ Date_____

A. Read the sentences. Find the places on the map. Work with a partner.

1. What state is north of Florida?

2. What state is south of Oklahoma?

3. What ocean is east of North America?

4. What country is south of Canada?

5. What state is south of Manitoba?

6. What country is north of the USA?

7. What state is south of Oregon?

8. What country is south of the USA?

9. What state is between California and Washington?

10. What province is next to Ontario?

11. What ocean is west of North America?

12. What province is north of Washington?

13. What state is next to Ontario?

14. What ocean is between Florida and Mexico?

B. How do you pronounce the names of these North American cities?

Boston   New York   Vancouver

Chicago   Los Angeles   Miami

Denver   San Francisco   Toronto

Houston   Seattle   Atlanta

Winnipeg   Washington D.C.

C. Where are they? Write the names on the map.

D. Write the weather under each picture.

It's sunny   **It's raining.**   **It's snowing.**
It's cloudy.   **It's windy.**   **It's foggy.**

1.

_____

2.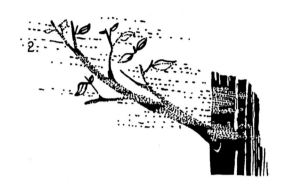

_____

3.

_____

4.

_____

5.

_____

6.

_____

Temperature

From Fahrenheit to Celsius (Centigrade)

EXAMPLE: 50°F = ?°C

1.	subtract 32 (– 32)	50 –32
2.	multiply by 5 (x 5)	18 x 5 = 90
3.	divide by 9 (÷ 9)	90 ÷ 9 = 10°C

From Celsius (Centigrade) to Fahrenheit

EXAMPLE: 10°C = ?°F

1.	multiply by 9 (x 9)	10 x 9 = 90
2.	divide by 5 (÷ 5)	90 ÷ 5 = 18
3.	add 32 (+ 32)	+32 = 50°F

E. Practice

1. 86°F = _____

2. 32°F = _____

3. 70°F = _____

4. 40°C = _____

5. 13°C = _____

6. 5°C = _____

What's the weather?   What's the temperature?

80°F and over	=	HOT
60° – 80°	=	WARM
40° – 60°	=	COOL
under 40°	=	COLD

What's the weather in _____?   It's _____.

What's the temperature in _____? It's _____. It's _____°.

EXAMPLE: What's the **weather** in Seattle? **It's raining.**

What's the **temperature** in Winnipeg? It's **cold**. It's **27°.**

F. Ask and answer questions about the cities on the map.

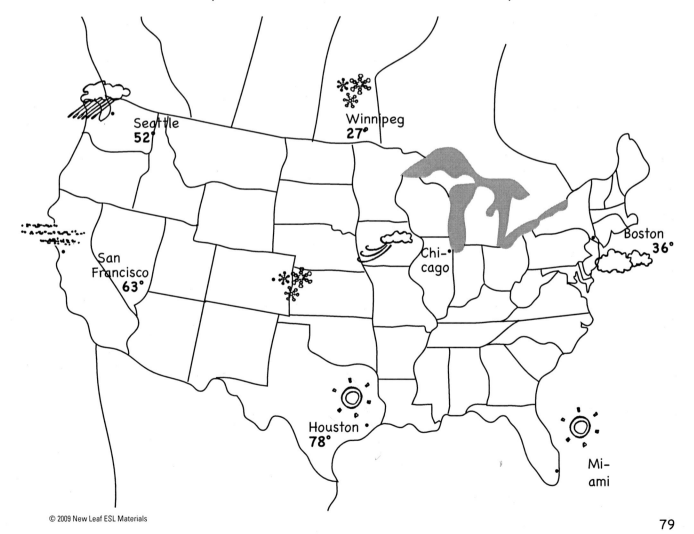

Vancouver 52°

Toronto .18°

New York 37°

Washington DC

Denver 40°

Los Angeles 82°

Atlanta 64°

G. Look at the map and answer these questions.

1. What's the weather in Toronto today? _____

2. Is it hot there today? _____

3. What's the temperature in Vancouver? _____

4. Is it snowing there ? _____

5. Is it raining in Washington D.C.? _____

6. What's the weather in Atlanta? _____

7. What's the temperature in Denver? _____

8. What's the weather in Los Angeles? _____

9. What's the temperature there? _____

10. Is it snowing in New York? _____

80

H. Look at the map and the answers and write questions.

1. _What's the weather in Atlanta?_ _____? It's sunny.

2. _____? It's warm. It's 64°.

3. _____? It's foggy.

4. _____? It's raining.

5. _____? It's cold. It's 37°.

6. _____? It's cloudy.

7. _____? It's cold. It's 18°.

8. _____? It's windy.

9. _____? It's hot. It's 82°.

10. _____? It's snowing.

I. Your town.

My town is _____.

1. What's the weather today?   _____

2. What's the temperature?   _____

J.

How many **syllables** are there? Where is the **stress**?

Listen to your teacher. Say the words.
Number the syllables. Underline the stress.

1. weather   2. Miami   3. temperature   4. Boston

5. Chicago   6. Toronto   7. thermometer   8. Seattle

CHAPTER 12

The Body and Health

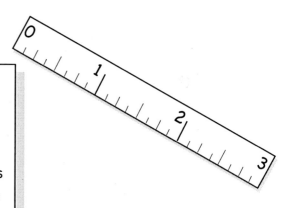

Measurement

1 foot (ft) = 12 inches (in)	1 foot = 30.48 cm
	1 inch = 2.54 cm
	1 pound = 454 grams
	1 kg = 2.205 pounds

A. What is their height? What is their weight?

1.   Mohammed is 6 feet 2 inches tall. He weighs 185 pounds. _____cm; _____kg

2.   Nadia is 5 feet 8 inches tall. She weighs 132 pounds.   _____cm; _____kg

3.   Soon is 5 feet 1 inch tall. She weighs 145 pounds.   _____cm; _____kg

4.   Carlos is 5 feet 11 inches tall. He weighs 190 pounds.   _____cm; _____kg

B. Use a ruler. Measure the things below in feet and inches.

1. How long is your thumb? _____

2. How long is your pinkie? _____

3. How long is your pencil or pen?_____

4. How long is your foot? _____

5. How long is your desk or table? _____

6. How high (tall) is your desk or table? _____

7. What size is this paper?   _____ X _____
                                        length   width

C. Measure these things in your house or apartment. Use feet and inches.

  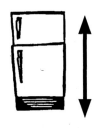

How long is your coffee table?   How long is your bed?   How tall is your refrigerator?

_____   _____   _____

How long is your sofa ?   How wide is your TV?

_____   _____

© 2009 New Leaf ESL Materials   83

Parts of the body

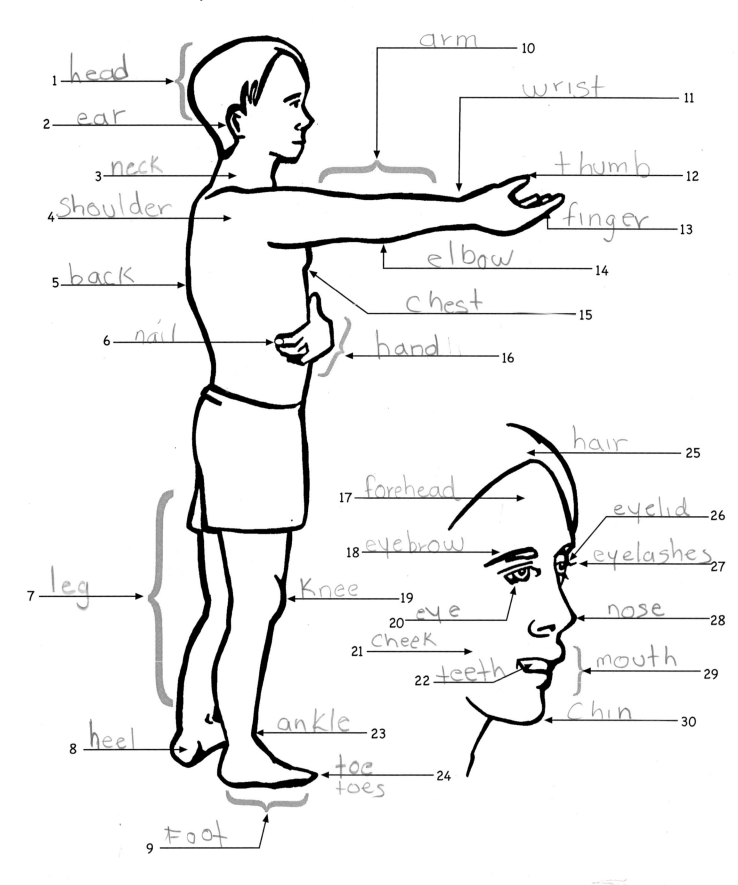

1 head
2 ear
3 neck
4 shoulder
5 back
6 nail
7 leg
8 heel
9 foot

10 arm
11 wrist
12 thumb
13 finger
14 elbow
15 chest
16 hand

17 forehead
18 eyebrow
19 knee
20 eye
21 cheek
22 teeth
23 ankle
24 toe toes
25 hair
26 eyelid
27 eyelashes
28 nose
29 mouth
30 chin

D. Write the name next to the picture.

ankle ✓	eye ✓	hand ✓	nose ✓
arm ✓	eyebrow ✓	head ✓	shoulder ✓
back ✓	eyelashes ✓	heel ✓	teeth
cheek ✓	eyelid ✓	knee ✓	thumb ✓
chest ✓	finger ✓	leg ✓	toe ✓
chin ✓	foot ✓	mouth ✓	wrist ✓
ear ✓	forehead ✓	nail ✓	
elbow ✓	hair ✓	neck ✓	

E. Write the body part in the sentence.

1. The _____Knee_____ is between the foot and the leg.

2. The _____back_____ is behind the chest.

3. The _____nose_____ is between the ears.

4. The _____forehead_____ is above the eyebrows.

5. The _____teeth_____ are in the mouth.

6. The _____mouth_____ is between the nose and the chin.

7. The _____Chest_____ is in front of the back.

8. The _____Wrist_____ is next to the thumb.

9. The _____eyelip_____ is under the eyebrow.

10. The _____Cheek_____ is next to the nose.

F. Going to the doctor. What do these words mean?

sick   appointment   clinic   receptionist
examination   shot   prescription   rest
medical record form   temperature

Jane's Trip to the Doctor.

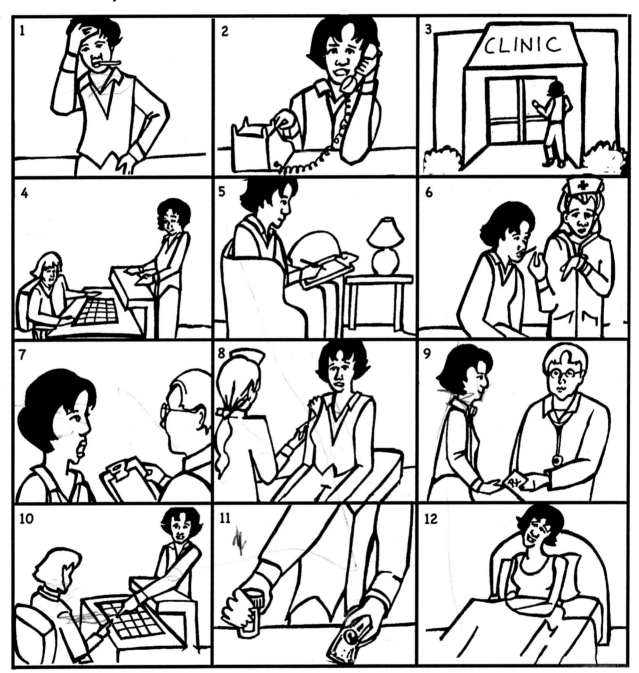

G. Look at the vocabulary. Look at the pictures.

   Match the number of the picture with the vocabulary.

   _11_ buy her prescription   _3_ go to the clinic

   _4_ check in with the receptionist   _6_ have her temperature taken

   _1_ feel sick   _7_ have an examination

   _5_ fill out a medical record form   _2_ make an appointment

   _9_ get a prescription from the doctor   _10_ make a return appointment

   _8_ get a shot   _12_ rest

H. Talk with your partner about each picture. Use the present continuous.

   EXAMPLE: ___Jane is feeling sick.___

I. Write a sentence about each picture. Use the present continuous.

1. _____Jane is feeling sick._____

2. _____Jane is making an appointment._____

3. _____Jane is going *to the clinic._____

4. _____Jane is checking in with the receptionist._____

5. _____Jane is filling out a medical record form._____

6. _____Jane is having an exa_____

7. _____

8. _Jenn_____

9. _____

10. _____

11. _____

12. _____Jane is resting_____

J. Write the name under the picture.

backache |0   headache ① (1)   earache   cut 9

sore throat 7   fever / temperature 8   high blood pressure   rash 4

toothache 3 || stomachache || sprain / swollen 2   bruise 5

1.

headache →migraña

2.

Sprain/swollen

3.

toothache

4.

rash

5.

bruise

6.

earache

7.

Sore throat

8.

fever/temperature

9.

cut

10.

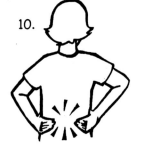

backache

11.

Stomachache

12.

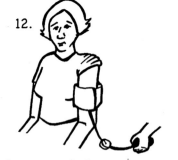

high blood pressure

88

K. Write the name under the picture.

pills/ tablets   crutches   eyedrops
bandage   cast   ice pack
Band-Aid   ointment   hot water bottle

1.

Pills / tablets

2.
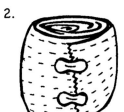
bandaje

3.

_____

4.

eyedrops

5.

Crutches

6.
_____
Ice Pack

7.

8.
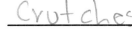

9.

_____   band - Aid   _____

L. Take this form home. Fill it out and bring it back to class.

MEDICAL FORM

Name_____
      Last   First   Middle Initial

Address _____
         Street   City   State   Zip

Social Security No. _____ Telephone_____

Birthdate _____ Birthplace _____ Marital Status _____

Sex   M   F   Age _____ Religion_____

Patient's Language_____ Interpreter Required?   Yes   No

Person to Notify _____ Relationship _____

Home Phone _____ Business Phone _____

Patient's Occupation _____

Patient's Workplace _____

Insurance company _____

Policy No. _____ Subscriber _____

Injury Information (if applicable) _____

Date/time injured _____ Place where injury occurred _____

HEALTH HISTORY Check the health problems you have had.

❑ Frequent colds   ❑ Bronchitis   ❑ Pneumonia
❑ Tuberculosis   ❑ Appendicitis   ❑ Asthma
❑ Diabetes   ❑ Cancer   ❑ Colitis
❑ Allergies   ❑ Fainting Spells ❑ Stomach Ulcer
❑ Migraines   ❑ Heart Attack   ❑ High Blood Pressure

Surgeries you have had   Medications you are taking   Allergies to Medication

_____   _____   _____

_____   _____   _____

_____   _____   _____

90

M. Look at the ad from Bob's Pharmacy. You and your partner have $8.00.

What can you buy?

1. Can you buy 12 rolls of toilet paper   Yes, we can.   No, we can't.
    and a toothbrush?

2. Can you buy a tube of toothpaste, shampoo,   Yes, we can.   No, we can't
    and a bar of soap?

3. Can you buy a bottle of lotion, a toothbrush   Yes, we can.   No, we can't
    and a tube of toothpaste?

4. Can you buy a bar of soap and   Yes, we can.   No, we can't
    and 12 rolls of toilet paper?

5. Can you buy a bottle of shampoo, a tube of toothpaste,
    and a bottle of lotion?   Yes, we can.   No, we can't.

6. How much is a tube of toothpaste, a toothbrush and a bar of soap? $_____

7. How much is a bottle of shampoo and 12 rolls of toilet paper? $_____

8. How much is a bar of soap, a toothbrush and a bottle of lotion? $_____

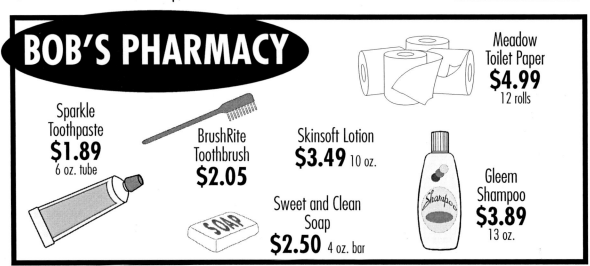

N.

How many syllables are there? Where's the stress?

Listen to your teacher. Say the words.
Number the syllables. Underline the stress.

1. bandage   2. appointment   3. ankle   4. bruise

5. sore throat 6. pharmacy   7. crutches   8. shoulder

9. inches   10. prescription   11. receptionist 12. shampoo

CHAPTER 13

Whose is it?

A. Our friends are at a carnival. Look at the picture.
   Can you find these things?

cotton candy   **Teddy bear**   **soda**   **tickets**   **hot dog**   **popcorn**

whose

> **Whose** purse is it?   It's **Soon's**.

B. Look at the picture and answer the questions.

1. Whose cotton candy is it?   _____

2. Whose Teddy bear is it?   _____

3. Whose child is he?   _____

4. Whose soda is it?   _____

5. Whose tickets are they?   _____

6. Whose glasses are they?   _____

7. Whose cap is it?   _____

8. Whose dog is it?   _____

9. Whose keys are they?   _____

10. Whose popcorn is it?   _____

C. Look at the answer. Make a question with <u>whose</u>.

EXAMPLE: *Whose Teddy bear is it?*   It's Carlos'.
          Whose keys are they?   They're Yuriy's.

1. _____ It's Soon's.

2. _____ They're Mohammed's.

3. _____ It's Nadia's.

4. _____ He's Jane's.

5. _____ They're Soon's.

6. _____ It's Nadia and Yuriy's.

7. _____ They're Yuriy's.

8. _____ It's Yuriy's.

Possessive Pronouns

You can take out the name and put in a pronoun:

Whose purse is it?   It's Soon's. = It's **hers**.

mine   yours   yours   theirs   his   hers   ours

D. Look at the picture. Make sentences from these words.

Use a name <u>or</u> a pronoun.

The	cap	Teddy bear	is	Carlos		his
	purse	cotton candy		Nadia	and	hers
	dog	glasses	are	Soon		theirs
	keys	tickets		Mohammed	's	
		popcorn		Jane		.
		hot dog		Joey		
				Yuriy		

1. _*The dog is Nadia and Yuriy's. The dog is theirs.*_____

2. _____

3. _____

4. _____

5. _____

6. _____

94

E. Talk with your partner. Give 4 answers to each question.

EXAMPLE: *Is that Nadia's cotton candy?*   *Yes, it's Nadia's candy.*

Yes, it's her candy.

Yes, it's Nadia's.

Yes, it's hers.

Are those Yuriy's tickets?   *No, they aren't Yuriy's tickets.*

No, they aren't his tickets.

No, they aren't Yuriy's.

No, they aren't his.

1. Is that Carlos' Teddy bear?

2. Are those Yuriy's keys?

3. Is that Joey's hot dog?

4. Are those Mohammed's glasses?

5. Is it Nadia and Yuriy's dog?

6. Is that Soon's popcorn?

F. Sit in a circle with 4 or 5 classmates.
Take something out of your pocket or purse.
Put it in the middle of your circle.
Ask and answer questions together.

EXAMPLE: *Whose pen is this?*   *It's Rosa's.*

It's mine.

It's hers.

Pronoun Review

I
me
my
mine

you
you
your
yours

you
you
your
yours

they
them
their
theirs

he
him
his
his

she
her
her
hers

we
us
our
ours

it
it

they
them

G. Put a pronoun in the blank.

1. That's Sally. _____ is a teacher.

2. There are about 35 students in Sally's class.

_____ are the students and Sally is _____ teacher.

3. _____ is a student.   _____ name is Yuriy.

Give the tickets to _____ .

4. _____ are students.

_____ names are Nadia and Yuriy.

Give the hot dogs to _____ .

96

5. My friend and I are students. _____ names are _____ and _____.

Give the popcorn to _____ .

6. _____ are glasses. Give _____ to Soon.

_____ are Soon's glasses. They are _____ .

7. _____ is a teddy bear.

Give _____ to Joey.

_____ is Joey's bear. It is _____ .

H. Fill in the blanks with

there   their   they're   theirs

1. _____ are about 275,000,000 people in the United States.

2. Ms. Henderson and Mr. Archer are _____ teachers.

3. This is my apartment. That one is _____.

4. _____ from Mexico.

5. Which car is _____?

6. Please put the extra chair over _____.

7. They can speak Russian, but _____ speaking English now.

8. We are going to _____ house for Thanksgiving.

CATALYNA

I. Put the words in the correct order.

1. pennies / give / Take / her / . / and / 3 / them / to

_____

2. keys / are/ Those / . / hers

_____

3. book / mine / these / yours / This / . / is / are / and / glasses

_____

4. quarters / is/ . / He / them / 2 / giving / to

_____

5. class / our / Is / ? / this

_____

6. our / are / These/ are / books / theirs / . / those / and

_____

7. teacher / and / We / theirs / are / listening / our / to / listening / they're / to / .

_____

8. some / him / She's / pencil / a / . / to / paper / giving / and

_____

98